AF279436

EBB
LEILA CHATTI

This is a work of fiction. All names, characters, places, and incidents are a product of the author's imagination. Any resemblance to real events or persons, living or dead, is entirely coincidental.

Published by Akashic Books
©2018 Leila Chatti

ISBN: 978-1-61775-633-7

All rights reserved
Printed in China through Four Colour Print Group, Louisville, Kentucky
First printing

Akashic Books
Brooklyn, New York, USA
Ballydehob, Co. Cork, Ireland
Twitter: @AkashicBooks
Facebook: AkashicBooks
E-mail: info@akashicbooks.com
Website: www.akashicbooks.com

African Poetry Book Fund
Prairie Schooner
University of Nebraska
110 Andrews Hall
Lincoln, Nebraska 68588

TABLE OF CONTENTS

Preface by Karen McCarthy Woolf 4

Postcard from Gone 7
Fasting in Tunis 8
of love, Sappho wrote 10
Dressing Before a Mirror in Morning 12
Indecision 14
Ramadan Lament 15
Waves 17
For a While I Understood Your Love 18
Faulty 19
On a Beach in Hergla, Five Months After 20
The Sadness Resumes Despite Beaches, Sun 22
Regimen 23
This Morning I Went to the Ocean to Feel 24
Now That You Are Gone 25
Autumn Aubade with Pigeons 26
Learning Again to Hunger 28
Walking Through Provincetown in January, I Fall in
Love Again 29
Postcard from Gone 30

Acknowledgments 32

PREFACE
by Karen McCarthy Woolf

Born to a Tunisian (Muslim) father and an American (Catholic) mother, Leila Chatti grew up as a dual citizen. Throughout her childhood she spent her winters in the US and summers in Tunisia. The Mediterranean was a constant and azure presence—a place of beauty and comfort, where the emotional and political impacts of today's refugee crisis had yet to make their mark. The rhythms of this cross-continental, cross-cultural fluidity are abiding in her work; as is the sea itself, as a physical entity, emotional template, and poetic protagonist.

With this in mind, if there is one word that captures the tone of these lithe and sonorous poems, it is the Portuguese term *saudade*. Although broadly considered untranslatable, it is proximate to melancholy, nostalgia —a sense of longing and loss, for a lover, a situation, or place. Historically, *saudade* is said to have been coined when the original colonials set sail for the New World, and the prospect of their never returning loomed large in the minds and hearts of those they left behind. Yet as a poetic construct, it is only partly elegiac, as it also describes something active, a presence of the absence itself.

A glance at the titles within *Ebb* confirms this association: most resonantly, "Postcard[s] from Gone," a pair of poems that open and close the collection; "Learning Again to Hunger," my personal favorite; "The Sadness Resumes Despite Beaches, Sun" and "Ramadan Lament," where the poet's dual heritage and concomitant religiosities merge in a tongue that Chatti describes elsewhere as "the muscle of heartache":

> I want to eat my grief and my god
> will not allow it. A lesson
> in suffering—*O!*
> *but Lord*—I have suffered.

I confess, I am
selfish, self-
absorbed—   […]

That heartache might be eternal, and possibly incurable; an agony that must be endlessly endured is the philosophical and narrative tension on which the collection hangs. This plays out variously, as in "Autumn Aubade with Pigeons," where loss becomes as absolute as extinction (which was the case for the once ubiquitous passenger pigeon to which the poem refers) and subsequently beneficial—as the sky brightens when the flocks dwindle. Then there are short, aphoristic poems such as "Indecision": ". . . I want /your lack so I might / require you—wish / you gone so / you can come back," which, with its epigraph from Adonis, gestures towards both the geography and sphere of Chatti's influences. Quotes from Robert Hass, Sappho, and Franz Wright constitute similar framing devices, while those not expressed by the author might include Yehuda Amichai and Louise Glück. I was interested to read that Chatti travels with a print copy of Glück's *Poems 1962-2012,* for there is a certain aspiration in the intensity of the lyric, rendered as much through omission as articulation.

Alongside yearning and desire, hunger is also a motif, both literal and figurative. For Chatti, the body is a site of multiple possibilities and pressures: an erogenous zone, where the actualities and politics of love and sex explode and contract, and alternately becomes a machine, which must ingest food to survive ("stale bread, a chocolate yogurt, / an artichoke stuffed with meat.") In "Regimen," a poem characterized by its capacity for metaphorically alert transformation, the poet's body becomes the sustenance it requires, as she "glaze[s her]self in early / sun like a pastry." Like the objects of her attention or thwarted desire, whether sea or lover, Chatti has the ability to shape-shift—to fruitfully utilize simile and metaphor to make something individual and urgent from a well-worn scenario.

The ascetic demands and subsequent rewards of religious abstention are another recurring and interlinked preoccupation: "I endure this day / as I have endured years of days / without the whole of your affection," she writes in "Fasting in Tunis," where the endurance that longing requires is tested in all its metaphorical and anthropomorphic guises: "The ocean eats and eats / at the sand and still hungers."

Despite these deprivations, there are no hardships to *endure* in this compelling, short collection, far from it. The poems within showcase a young poet whose voice carries with it an enviable combination of gravitas and passion. If love's hazards are a test, they are also cyclical. In "Learning Again to Hunger" the speaker brings a new man with her to the beach— "to sit at the edge of the earth," a phrase that recalls *saudade* as an emotion that begins and ends with its subject gazing out to the horizon. When the poet's companion offers her half a sandwich, there's grit in it, but she eats it nonetheless.

POSTCARD FROM GONE

When you left I walked
into the ocean. Not to
drown but to be held

by something
reluctant
to let go. Don't

make this bigger
than it is, which is big
enough to swallow

whales
and civilizations.
I joined

the blue, I was blue.
And when I looked
down, I shattered

and reformed
so many times, you know, I couldn't catch
a clear look at myself.

FASTING IN TUNIS

*"Longing, we say, because desire is full
of endless distances."*
　　—Robert Hass

My God taught me hunger
is a gift, it sweetens
the meal. All day, I have gone without
because I know at the end I will
eat and be satisfied. In this way,
my desire is bearable.

I endure this day
as I have endured years of days
without the whole of your affection.
Your desire is one capable of rest.
Mine keeps its eyes open, stalks
through heat that quivers,
waits to be fed.

The sun burns a hole through
the sky and I am patient.
The ocean eats and eats
at the sand and still hungers.
I watch its wide blue tongue, knowing
you are on the other side.

What is greater: the distance between
these bodies or their need?

Noon gapes, a vacant maw—
there is long to go
until the moon is served, white as a plate.
You are far and still sleeping;
the morning has not yet slunk into your bed,
its dreams so vast and solitary.

Once, long ago,
I touched you,
and I will touch you again—
your mouth a song
I remember, your mouth
a sugar I drink.

OF LOVE, SAPPHO WROTE

sweetbitter—and of course

the tongue is the muscle
of heartache, the one

which defines as separate
territories of the body—

throat and lip and ridge
of pelvic bone, nipple pink

as dawn in the mouth—
I have tasted

surfacing your garland
of hair, salt, you have come

to my well and drank—
if again you leave,

leave fully, for
the return is grief

of an acute kind—
last I saw you summer

pulsed like a fever, you came
and I fed you

blackberries in bed,
dark swallows

of sweetness—
I stained your body

with each kiss—

DRESSING BEFORE A MIRROR IN MORNING

I look at myself
because it is what you would do, it makes me
feel close to you.

For months only your silence
for company—the lack,
in that way, reliable.
It hovers too long
like a man in the room.

Light from the window slips its flush
fingers under my blouse.
At my hip, gold hairs rise
like good pupils. The mirror bright

and eager as an eye.
I have learned to be

a watched thing

through years
of your gaze, you who claimed

you could stay
hours waiting for the flash
of my skin between
buttons, who took

such clear pleasure in it.
I felt

like a god, or at least a woman
one might love
into suffering.

I fix myself
in that stare. As if I were, as you saw me
once, vital—

a being worthy
of worship, terror.

INDECISION

> *"Ah, go on, move. No, wait, you're*
> *not leaving, are you?"*
> —Adonis

If you go and I have not
asked you to go,
it is the worst thing. But if
I go (thus rendering you
One Who is Left), this is bearable, almost
pleasurable, the act
of leaving—but never
after, reflecting,
at rest. I want you
gone but I am unwilling
to relinquish you. I want
your lack so I might
require you—wish
you gone so
you can come back.

RAMADAN LAMENT

"There is courtship, and there is hunger."
　　—Mary Szybist

I want to eat my grief and my god
will not allow it. A lesson
in suffering—*O!*
but Lord—I have suffered.

I confess, I am
selfish, self-
absorbed—I consume

so I might rid myself
of what

I want through its destruction.

Before me as barrier, the ocean
swallowing, no
regard for consequence—in my grief
let me be simple like that.

My mouth, without
the other's: useless.
I long to fill it like a grave.

O Lord,
don't speak
to me

of restraint—I have abstained

so devoutly
in your name I am

defined by that absence, so long
I am wasting away.

WAVES

Do you remember, when you wanted
to fuck me, you wrote the word
undulate? So the waves appear

all vulgar to me now.
I watched once
a video of boys

moving like water
over a sofa, the floor, walls, looking
to prove themselves

adequate
lovers with nothing
to love. Maybe you

were like this—devoted
to the verb without
context, without a body

to wash up against.
Here, even the air
ripples. You can see it

writhing on
the horizon. If you look long enough
you can see in it

anything you wish.

FOR A WHILE I UNDERSTOOD YOUR LOVE

as water, sand.
Limitless, and so

something
I could possess

a part of. But each
time I got

my hands on it, it slipped
through—

I grasped and grasped
and it slipped faster.

FAULTY

Because I was not loved
I wanted to be loved, I was sure
I would die without it.

Which is, of course, faulty
logic—I was living
through it, so it did not kill me.

Only I could kill me,
which, of course, I tried.
Which didn't help my case.

I wanted to be loved more
than I wanted to be
alive. For so long

I thought not *to be*
loved is good but *to be loved*
is to be *good.*

All those years, convinced—*surely*
I must be bad, the way
you keep punishing me.

ON A BEACH IN HERGLA, FIVE MONTHS AFTER

"He's not in the hospital now,
the hospital's in him."
　　—Franz Wright

Noon sun a white bulb.
　　　　Here, we say *close*

the light like a door.
　　　　Still I feel shut

out of myself
　　　　　as if visiting

an old haunt:
　　　　strange tenant, new

trimmings. Whose
　　　　body displayed

for God's weary stare?
　　　　The ocean whispers,

but I see its blue scar.
　　　　There are days

my life feels like a gift
　　　　I'm not sure

I won't return.

There are others I wake

glad for diligent
        mornings which enter

uninvited like light
        shone through the door

every quarter hour. I'm alive,
        as if it were simple,

and the sun continues
        doing its rounds.

THE SADNESS RESUMES DESPITE BEACHES, SUN

I try to shock myself
into obedience as I would
a bad child. *You could be
dead!* and *isn't it marvelous?*—
my chest rising
beneath my blouse like dough.

It's miserable to be
miserable when confined by
such obstinate beauty.
Spume effervescent
as soda pop. Palms
blonde as towheads
lining the road.

I try, believe me, to rise
and accept the sun's sweet
praise. It returns
at my door like a stray
I'm unkind to.

I try, I try, but
all day the light paws
at a door I can't answer.

REGIMEN

Yes, I know the routine.

I sleep the requisite eight hours
then take a nap,
for good measure.

I eat more
or less

three meals—stale bread, a chocolate yogurt,
an artichoke stuffed with meat.

Mornings, I glaze myself in early
sun like a pastry
and drift

back and forth in the pool, head above water,
as sand hisses by and sparrows
dive in for a drink.

Twenty-six years I have managed to stay
alive, and I make it look so ordinary.

Some days, I even forget
there's an option. It's habit

now, the dull labor,
my heart clanging away for so long
I'm resigned, I might as well let it.

THIS MORNING I WENT TO THE OCEAN TO FEEL

sorry for myself. I wanted to
see it from your side. For years, stood
on that other shore imagining
the distance endless,
so as not to understand you
simply would not cross. Boats
bobbed, tethered, and shook
at me their masts as if
disappointed. There I go
again, anchoring myself
at the center. The truth is,
I wept and no one noticed.
It was not beautiful nor profound.
All this time I've wasted.
Fog eased from the horizon, and the waves
dribbled toward my feet.

NOW THAT YOU ARE GONE

I walk the shore and kiss a man and all is black—the sand, the sky, the water

gnawing toward me, black.

I say *I've never seen anything more beautiful* and can't see a thing.

Your name washes up like glass, the edges dulled.

Your name brine in the eye of my mouth.

My grief slow and plodding, as many times I've struggled against the surf.

Your face an image bled by time and water.

I float and call it survival.

I swallow the salt of a man and call it love.

I try to write but my language bleeds before it reaches you.

I try to write but my language bleeds.

My grief an image. My mouth dulled.

I try to write *you are gone, many years* but slip—

you are gone, many tears.

AUTUMN AUBADE WITH PIGEONS

*"When an individual is seen gliding through the woods
and close to the observer, it passes like a thought, and on
trying to see it again, the eye searches in vain; the bird
is gone."*
        — John James Audubon, 'The Passenger Pigeon"

Early orange cold in my lap, drinking
tea and sucking the honeyed spoon,
I heard them: coos like groans,
I thought them lovers in another house.

All these solitary gilded mornings
with the bruise-necked birds.
How long since last your breath
stirred the wisps at my nape

to wake me?
            I flew an ocean to escape you.

Overhead, pigeons like a thought
settling. One

dove, a shadow past the window.

            *Still unsummoned
            you flutter back.*

Once the sky blackened with birds
for miles, dusky swathes of living cloud,

a thousand wings thundering.
I can't imagine it, looking up
into the sudden dark

or the swell of sun returning
like a second, clumsy dawn—

> *I loved so much I thought*
> *I would never see around it—*

but long ago the skies were emptied.
Unobstructed, the light tumbles in.

LEARNING AGAIN TO HUNGER

I watch the tide like once I watched
my mother. To learn from it. To learn how
better to hunger, how to want
like a woman—insistent, insatiable. Just
when I think I've escaped
its reach, it slinks forward, swallows
the toe of my boot. It's still
winter and my breath
is obvious as adolescence
but I've brought a man with me
to sit at the edge of the earth.
I needed to
see the edge shift
right before my eyes
to convince me there's no end
to hunger. We share
a blanket and a meal and brace against
the cold. It's so cold
the water looks almost silver
and the sky's
wiped blank. The edge
approaches then recedes, reveals
its glossy detritus. He offers me
half a sandwich. When I bite down
there's grit. I eat it.

WALKING THROUGH PROVINCETOWN IN JANUARY, I FALL IN LOVE AGAIN

with my life. The fleece of it
draped silver midair. From the eaves of houses,
icicles dripping, keeping
time with my pulse.
(How could I have ever wanted
to cut you out? Bluest
ribbon of my blood
looped around my wrist as if a finger, so as not
to forget—) Through the haze, sun-
break demanding as a child. Messy dayglow on
slush, spilling everywhere like milk.
I pause at the harbor, its broad
clean slate. My cheeks
red as the first day. My feet planted
at the edge, lapped by the swash like kisses.

POSTCARD FROM GONE

I've found a shore
I never loved you
on, and so

the world again feels new.
I could tell you
so many things

if I wanted to tell you
anything. I could tell you
there's a fox who sleeps

with the dead and dunes
shifting constantly
like truths. I carry

sand in every fold
of my clothing. When I undress,
there's a sound

like whispers.
I could tell you
I've learned to

love the dark
that swells
so early and stays

so long. I could tell you

I've stopped speaking
all day to you

and calling it myself.

ACKNOWLEDGMENTS

The author would like to thank the editors of the following journals in which these poems first appeared:

diode: "Waves," "Now That You Are Gone"
Fifth Wednesday Journal: "This Morning I Went to the Ocean to Feel," "Learning Again to Hunger"
The Los Angeles Review: "Ramadan Lament"
Narrative Magazine: "Fasting in Tunis"
Poetry Northwest: "Dressing Before a Mirror in Morning"
Prairie Schooner: "Indecision," "Faulty"
Spoon River Poetry Review: "Autumn Aubade with Pigeons"
Southword Journal: "of love, Sappho wrote"
The Shallow Ends: "Postcard from Gone"
wildness: "Postcard from Gone," "Walking Through Provincetown in January, I Fall in Love Again"

Deep gratitude to the creative writing program at North Carolina State University, the Munster Literature Centre, Dickinson House, the Tin House Writers' Workshop, the Fine Arts Work Center in Provincetown, and the Wisconsin Institute for Creative Writing for their generous funding and support;

Dorianne Laux, Mary Szybist, Anita Skeen, Joy Harjo, Emilia Phillips, Deryn Rees-Jones, Kwame Dawes, Chris Abani, Rebecca Bornstein, Carlene Kucharczyk, Laura Thorp, Elizabeth Purvis, Tayler Heuston, Emily Rose Cole, Allison DeVille, Philip Matthews, Naya Bricher, and Kristen Ratzsch for their encouragement, guidance, and friendship;

Hend Ben Salah for late nights and long conversations by the water;

and Henrik Mader, Michael Deagler, Clay Reimann, Bryce Emley, Samuel Piccone, Erin Willie, Lexi Wilson, and Elissa Fountain for keeping me afloat.